Book 1
Excel Shortcuts

BY SAM KEY

&

Book 2
PHP Programming Professional Made Easy

BY SAM KEY

Book 1

Excel Shortcuts

BY SAM KEY

The 100 Top Best Powerful Excel Keyboard Shortcuts in 1 Day!

Programming Box Set #72: Excel Shortcuts & PHP Programming Professional Made Easy

Table Of Contents

Introduction

I want to thank you and congratulate you for purchasing the book, "The Power of Excel Shortcuts: The 100 Top Best Powerful Excel Keyboard Shortcuts in 1 Day!".

This book contains proven steps and strategies on how to master the Microsoft Excel through just 100 keyboard shortcuts! However, most people will ask, "Why do you need to learn these shortcuts anyway?"

Advantages of Using Microsoft Excel

Microsoft Excel has become one of the most commonly used enterprise software in schools and offices. Its way of presenting data, which is through a spreadsheet, has helped a lot of people especially in the field of data mining. If you were going to put numerous rows of data, in let's say, a word processing program, it might take a lot of time creating tables and formatting each of them to fit in the pages. With the Microsoft Excel, these manual tasks are now much easier.

What does the Microsoft Excel have that other programs don't? For one, it has a built-in spreadsheet that you can manipulate the size and formatting. This versatile way of maneuvering the spreadsheet made it indispensable for many. Now, gone are the days were people have to manually draw tables in sheets of paper. Excel has already the tables prepared for them.

Another nifty feature of this software is its calculation function. Excel houses a myriad of formulas for solving arithmetic, financial and logical problems, among others. Thus, one doesn't even need to calculate every sum or average of a data series. Just by using a formula in Excel, everything can be done in an instant.

The Secret behind Mastering Excel

Speaking of instant, did you know that Excel has more than a hundred keyboard shortcuts? What does this mean to you as an Excel user? It means you can continuously work on your Excel spreadsheet without having to depend on your mouse constantly for Excel functions.

This is especially helpful whenever you are inputting a lot of data, and doing this will be more efficient if both of your hands weren't switching from keyboard to mouse and vice versa, every once in a while. In addition, if your mouse suddenly chose the most inopportune time to malfunction, learning Excel shortcuts can save you from major headaches.

As such, this book will provide you 100 keyboard shortcuts which you can use in Excel. In addition, as a bonus, you will learn about alternatives in case you forget any of these shortcuts.

Thanks again for purchasing this book, I hope you enjoy it!

Chapter 1: Moving Around the Excel Screen

People typically use the mouse for navigating the Excel screen. With this device, you can manipulate every cell in Excel, including its formatting and color. Since the mouse can access the major functions in Excel through the ribbon, there is no need for you to manually-type every formula or command.

However, the only difficult thing that you cannot do with a mouse is entering text. If you're going to use an on-screen keyboard, keying in the data in every cell would probably take you a lot longer than just using the keyboard for the text.

Thus, if you're going to use the keyboard most of the time, especially if you're just starting to build the spreadsheet data from scratch, it would be helpful to learn the basic keyboard shortcuts for moving around the Excel spreadsheet.

Shortcut #1: Arrow Keys

There are four arrow keys found in the right side of your main keyboard keys. These are the Arrow Left, Arrow Right, Arrow Up, and Arrow Down keys. Intuitively, you know that you can use these keys for moving within the spreadsheet. For instance, by selecting a cell then pressing Arrow Up, it will situate the cursor in the cell directly above your selected cell.

Shortcut #2: Ctrl + Arrow Key

Let's assume that you have a block of Excel data that spans more than 50,000 rows and more than 200 columns. You would probably have a hard time using a mouse in skimming these voluminous data. As such, you can use the Ctrl + Arrow key to navigate each "ends" of the data easily. In this example, click any cell in the block of data then press Ctrl + Arrow Down. You will be immediately located to the bottom cell in that specific column.

Shortcut #3: Shift + Arrow Key

You have selected all the items in the row but you forgot to include one cell. What would you do if you needed to include the next cell in the selection? Simply press Shift + Arrow Key, where the arrow pertains to the direction of the region you want to highlight.

Shortcut #4: Ctrl + Shift + Arrow Key

The above shortcut only includes one cell in the selection; but what would happen if you want to include everything until the last cell containing a data? You then use the Ctrl + Shift + Arrow Key.

Shortcut #5: Backspace

The Backspace key immediately deletes the contents of the active cell. However, if the cell is in Edit mode, it will only delete one character in the left of the insertion point, or the blinking cursor in the Formula bar.

Shortcut #6: Delete

This key has the same function as the Backspace key. However, instead of the left side, it removes a character in the right hand side of the insertion point.

Shortcut #7: End

Pressing the End key will enable the End Mode in Excel. In this mode, if you press an Arrow key, it will directly take you to the last used cell (or if none, last cell) in that specific direction. However, if the Scroll Lock is on, pressing the End key will only take you to the lower right corner of your Excel screen.

Shortcut #8: Ctrl + End

It works the same as the End key where pressing this combination will take you to the last used cell. However, if no cells were used, it will not move to the end of the worksheet like the End key does. Also, if the insertion point is located in the Formula bar (e.g., after the first character), Ctrl + End will put this cursor at the end of the field.

Shortcut #9: Ctrl + Shift + End

This keyboard shortcut can do two functions. First, in the Formula bar, it will select every character at the right of the insertion point. On the other hand, if you use it in the worksheet, it will highlight the cells starting from the active cell (or selected cell) until the last used cell in the worksheet.

Shortcut #10: Spacebar

Aside from putting a space in your text, it can also either select or clear a checkbox.

Shortcut #11: Ctrl + Spacebar

This will select the whole column to where the active cell is located.

Shortcut #12: Shift + Spacebar

It has the same function as the above, but this shortcut selects rows instead of columns.

Shortcut #13: Ctrl + Shift + Spacebar

Pressing these keys will select your entire worksheet.

Shortcut #14: Enter

After you have entered a data in a cell, pressing the Enter key will complete the input of data. Besides that, you can also directly go one cell below through this key. Considered as the most commonly used shortcut in Excel, you will be using the Enter key quite a lot because all Excel functions need it.

Shortcut #15: Shift + Enter

If you press Enter, you will go down one cell. Conversely, a Shift + Enter will complete an entry in a cell but the cursor will go directly above your entry.

Shortcut #16: Ctrl + Enter

Since this is a spreadsheet, it follows that after you have put an entry, you will enter another data below it. That is the common task whenever you're working on a table or database, which explains why the Enter key goes down. However, if you think that you need the downward movement, you can try Ctrl + Enter. This will plainly enter your data in the cell and it won't move your cursor to another direction.

Shortcut #17: Alt + Enter

You want the data to go into the next line in the same cell. However, if you press Enter, the cursor just moves on to the next cell in line. Pressing the Tab key doesn't work either. So what will you do? Try Alt + Enter key and see if it works.

Shortcut #18: Esc Key

The Escape key, or simply "Esc", performs a lot of nifty functions in Excel. Among of which are the following: 1) deletes a whole data in a cell, 2) exits you from a dialog box, and 3) escapes you from the full screen mode of Excel.

Shortcut #19: Home Key

The Home key will take you to the first cell in the specific row of your active cell. However, if the Scroll Lock is on, the cursor will go to the upper-left corner of your current window.

Shortcut #20: Ctrl + Home

This shortcut, also known as the "True Home key", brings the user to the beginning of the worksheet.

Shortcut #21: Ctrl + Shift + Home

This will select all cells from the active cell up to the first cell in the worksheet.

Shortcut #22: Page Down

Scouring among rows and rows of worksheets is now easy because of this button. This will display the next page in your Excel window.

Shortcut #23: Alt + Page Down

Unlike Page Down, the Alt + Page Down combination will show the next page to the right of your current window.

Shortcut #24: Ctrl + Page Down

Flipping in several worksheets is now easy thanks to Ctrl + Page Down. This will automatically turn you over to the next worksheet.

Shortcut #25: Ctrl + Shift + Page Down

The normal way of selecting several worksheets at once is to hold Ctrl while clicking each of the worksheets to be included in the selection.

However, for those who don't think this is the practical way to do it, here's an alternative. Use the Ctrl + Shift + Page Down; it will automatically select the sheets for you.

Shortcut #26: Page Up

This is quite similar to Shortcut #22: Page Down key, except for the fact that this one goes in the opposite direction (which is upward).

Shortcut #27: Alt + Page Up

The Alt + Page Up will move your screen to the left, instead of right as what was described in Shortcut #23: Alt + Page Down.

Shortcut #28: Ctrl + Page Up

Same as Shortcut #24: Ctrl + Page Down, this will enable you to change sheets easily. However, this one goes in a counterclockwise direction.

Shortcut #29: Ctrl + Shift + Page Up

Selecting sheets is also a function of the Ctrl + Shift + Page Up. However, it will select the worksheets on the left hand side of your current sheet first.

Shortcut #30: Tab Key

Using the Tab key will enable you to move to the right hand side of the cell. Also, if you have a protected worksheet, pressing this can immediately take you to the next unlocked cell. Lastly, in case there is a dialog box, you can easily move along the options through the Tab key.

Shortcut #31: Shift + Tab

The Shift + Tab works the opposite way; if pressing Tab will take you to the right hand cell, this shortcut will locate the left cell for you. It also applies to the other functions of the Tab key. In a dialog box for instance, keying in Shift + Tab will move you to the previous option.

Shortcut #32: Ctrl + Tab

You're now done with shortcuts for moving around cells and worksheets. As such, the succeeding shortcuts in this chapter will focus on dialog boxes. For this shortcut, use it if you want to go to the next tab in a dialog box.

Shortcut #33: Ctrl + Shift + Tab

However, if you wish to go back to the previous tab in a dialog box, using the Ctrl + Shift + Tab is the right combination.

So there you have it, the first 33 keyboard shortcuts in Excel. Hopefully, through these tips you can know traverse in your multitude of cells and worksheets with no difficulty at all.

Chapter 2: Navigating the Excel Ribbon

Microsoft created the "ribbon" as a replacement to the expanding menus in the earlier versions of Microsoft Excel. It houses all the functions in Excel such as formatting, page layout, pictures, and shapes. However, since its interface is not in an expanding menu style, people are not that familiar with its keyboard shortcuts as compared to before where you can immediately see which shortcut runs which.

To help you with that, here are some of the most commonly used keyboard shortcuts for exploring the Ribbon.

Shortcut #34: Alt Key

Letters and numbers will appear in the ribbon once you push the Alt key. What happens is that it activates the access keys, wherein typing in corresponding letter or number will let you select a specific function in the ribbon.

Shortcut #35: F10

This key has the same function as the Alt key, only that pressing the F10 would require you to use your right hand instead.

Shortcut #36: Alt + Arrow Left/Right

To be able to navigate to the other tabs, use these keys.

Shortcut #37: F10 + Arrow Left/Right

Since it was previously mentioned that the F10 behaves the same way as the Alt key, pressing F10 followed by an arrow to the left or to the right will also transfer you to other tabs.

Shortcut #38: Ctrl + F1

There's no doubt that the ribbon indeed takes up quite a lot of space in your screen. Therefore, for those who want more area for their spreadsheet, hiding the ribbon is the best option. To do that, simply press Ctrl + F1. To show the ribbon again, also press the same shortcut.

Shortcut #39: Shift + F10

Shift + F10 is similar to the right click button of your mouse. It can open menus and other options depending on where your cursor is.

Shortcut #40: F6

You can move along three areas of the screen through this key. The F6 key, will take you either to the ribbon, the spreadsheet, or the status bar.

Shortcut #41: F10 + Tab

In a tab, you can browse through the functions by pressing this combination continuously. You can also press this shortcut first, and then proceed with the arrow keys for navigation.

Shortcut #42: F10 + Shift + Tab

The above shortcut goes around the functions in a clockwise manner. On the contrary, the F10 + Shift + Tab shortcut does otherwise.

Shortcut #43: F1

In the upper right corner of the ribbon, there is a blue question mark icon. Accessing this icon will take you to the Microsoft Excel Help task pane. Alternatively, if you press F1 the same pane will open.

Since the area around the ribbon is limited, it is only appropriate that there would be less keyboard shortcuts dedicated for it. All in all, there are ten button combinations for the ribbon.

Chapter 3: Formatting the Excel Spreadsheet

If you're also a user of the Microsoft Word, you are probably familiar with formatting keyboard shortcuts such as Ctrl + B, which stands for bold text or Ctrl + I, which italicizes your text. Since you can do almost every basic feature that you need in the Word application through the keyboard, this makes the formatting easier for you.

Fortunately, even though Excel is not a word-processing program, it also has dedicated keyboard shortcuts that for formatting. These are as follows:

Shortcut #44: Alt + ‘

By going to the Styles group in the Home tab, you can quickly change the appearance of the cell by selecting any of the pre-installed styles in Excel. To see the formatting changes done within a cell, you click on the New Style option, which will take you to the Style dialog box. Similarly, clicking Alt + ‘ will get you in the same menu.

Shortcut #45: Ctrl + B

Like in Microsoft Word, Ctrl + B will either apply or remove a bold format in a text.

Shortcut #46: Ctrl + 2

This shortcut can also make the selected text into a bold type.

Shortcut #47: Ctrl + I

Letter I stands for Italics. As such, clicking Ctrl + I will turn any text into an italicized type.

Shortcut #48: Ctrl + 3

This also functions like the Ctrl + I shortcut.

Shortcut #49: Ctrl + U

Ctrl + U will put an underline in the selected text.

Shortcut #50: Ctrl + 4

Another alternative for the Ctrl +U is the Ctrl + 4 shortcut.

Shortcut #51: Ctrl + 5

To easily put a strikethrough in your text, press Ctrl + 5.

Shortcut #52: Ctrl + Shift + F

If you want more font formatting options, you can just proceed to the Font tab of the Format cells dialog box. Right-clicking a cell then selecting Format Cells will get you there, or you can just use this shortcut.

Shortcut #53: Ctrl + Shift + P

This shortcut works the same as the above.

Shortcut #54: Ctrl + Shift + &

Now that you're done with editing the text, this shortcut as well as the succeeding ones will pertain to cell formatting. As for Ctrl + Shift + &, it will put a plain black border on all sides of the cell.

Shortcut #55: Ctrl + Shift + _

On the contrary, Ctrl + Shift + _ will remove the borders that you have made.

Shortcut #56: F4

Instead of manually doing all the formatting for a number of cells, Excel has a shortcut wherein you can redo the formatting that you just did in another cell. This is the F4 function key. For example, if you have put borders in Cell A1, selecting Cell A2 then pressing F4 will also create borders for that specific cell.

Shortcut #57: Ctrl + 1

Pressing the Ctrl + 1 will show the Format Cells dialog box. In this box, you can edit every possible formatting for a cell such as number format, alignment, font, border, and fill.

The previous chapters have discussed how certain shortcuts can perform specific functions in Excel such as formatting cells and navigating the spreadsheet. In the following chapters, the topics will be about the different uses of specific buttons such as the Function keys and the Control key.

Chapter 4: Working with Function Keys

The first row of keys in your keyboard contains the function keys, which is denoted by the letter F followed by a number. In the Windows desktop, these function keys can do a variety of tasks such as adjusting the screen brightness or minimizing the volume.

Excel uses the function keys for different purposes. Thus, most people usually have a difficulty mastering the Function key shortcuts in Excel.

Shortcut #58: Alt + F1

Alt + F1 will automatically create a chart for you. Just select the range of cells containing your chart data then press this shortcut. Afterwards, a column chart will appear in the worksheet.

Shortcut #59: Alt + Shift + F1

The normal way in creating a new worksheet is by right-clicking any of the existing worksheets then choosing Insert. The same task can be done by this shortcut.

Shortcut #60: F2

In editing a formula, you can't just simply select an active cell; you have to click on the Formula bar so that you can make changes to it. Fortunately, the F2 will put the cell in Edit mode. Thus, if you want to amend a cell, there's no need for you to click on the Formula bar; just use F2 instead.

Shortcut #61: Shift + F2

The Shift + F2 shortcut will insert comments in the active cell.

Shortcut #62: Ctrl + F2

Unlike the previous F2 combinations, this one has nothing to do with editing a cell. When you press Ctrl + F2, you will be forwarded to the Print Preview screen. Upon exiting this screen, your spreadsheet will show dotted lines which serves as a marker for a page border.

Shortcut #63: F3

Instead of constantly referring to a range of cells by their cell location (e.g., A1:D1), you can just define a name for this range. Thus, whenever you want to pertain to that specific range in a formula, you can simply put its name; there's no need for you to put the cell range. F3 will take you to the Paste Name dialog box, wherein you can list all the names created in a worksheet and their respective cell references.

Shortcut #64: Ctrl + F3

To create a new name, go to the Name Manager through Ctrl + F3.

Shortcut #65: Shift + F3

Using formulas is the heart of Microsoft Excel. Without it, you cannot do any calculations in the spreadsheet. As such, there is a dedicated tab for Formulas in the Excel ribbon. However, it may take quite a lot of time for users to efficiently look for the appropriate formula with all the possible options in the Formulas tab. Because of this, the Shift + F3 key combination is made. It opens the Insert Function dialog box, wherein you can easily search for a formula by just typing in the description of what you need to do.

Shortcut #66: Ctrl + F4

You don't need to click that "X" mark in the upper left corner of your Excel screen just to close the application; a simple Ctrl + F4 is enough to do the job.

Shortcut #67: F5

Rummaging through a lot of cells takes a lot of work, especially if you're dealing with thousands of rows in a spreadsheet. The Go To dialog box, which can be accessed through F5, will help you reach that specific cell or range that you wanted to see.

Shortcut #68: Ctrl + F5

By default, all workbooks are always in full screen mode in Excel. However, if you're doing work on several Excel files at once, it may be hard to switch from one file to the other when each workbook is on full screen. Through Ctrl + F5, the selected file restore to window size in the Excel screen so that you can easily switch across files.

Shortcut #69: Shift + F6

This works the same as Shortcut #40: F6, albeit in a counterclockwise direction.

Shortcut #70: Ctrl + F6

If you have more than one workbook open, pressing Ctrl + F6 will let you switch among these workbooks.

Shortcut #71: F7

Aside from Microsoft Word, the Excel application has also a built-in spell checker. To check the spelling of every word in your spreadsheet, press F7. This will run the Spelling dialog box. Apart from detecting erroneous spellings, it also suggests possible words that can replace the incorrect word.

Shortcut #72: Ctrl + F7

As mentioned before, you should not use the full screen mode when working with several Excel files. This is so that you can select each workbook with ease. The Ctrl + F7 shortcut executes the Move command so that you can drag the unneeded workbooks in another area in the Excel screen where it can't obstruct your view.

Shortcut #73: F8

Upon pressing F8, the Excel goes into an Extend Selection mode. This enables you to use the arrow keys to extend the current selection. Pressing the same key will also lift the Extend Selection mode.

Shortcut #74: Shift + F8

The limitation of the F8 key is that it only adds adjacent cells in the selection. Through Shift + F8, you can now add any nonadjacent cell by using arrow keys.

Shortcut #75: Ctrl + F8

To resize your workbook, use Ctrl + F8. This will run the Size command for workbooks that are not in a full screen mode.

Shortcut #76: Alt + F8

A macro is a set of actions created using the Visual Basic programming language. What it does is to automate a set of tasks in Excel. For example, you're going to retrieve a data in a one sheet then you'll paste the said data in another sheet. However, if you're going to do the copy-paste task for thousands of data, it might take you a long time. As such, you can use the macro for this. Alt + F8 will open the Macro dialog box, where you can record and run a macro.

Shortcut #77: F9

This is the Refresh button in Excel. Once you refresh a workbook, it will recalculate all new formulas in the said file.

Shortcut #78: Shift + F9

On the other hand, Shift + F9 will only recalculate the formulas in the worksheet you are currently working on.

Shortcut #79: Ctrl + Alt + F9

This has the same function as F9, but it will also recalculate formulas that have not been changed.

Shortcut #80: Ctrl + Alt + Shift + F9

Aside from doing what the Ctrl + Alt + F9 shortcut does, it also rechecks all dependent formulas for any errors.

Shortcut #81: Alt + Shift + F10

Smart tags are data that are labeled in a particular type. For instance, a person's name in an Outlook email message can be labeled with this tag. You can open the smart tag menu through this shortcut.

Shortcut #82: Ctrl + F10

This will enable a workbook to display in full screen mode (or maximized mode).

Shortcut #83: F11

The Shortcut #58: Alt + F1 will let you create charts by highlighting the data series. Similarly, the F11 key has the same function except that you don't need to select the data series; it will automatically detect the data for you. Another difference between these two shortcuts is that the Alt + F1 will display the chart in the same worksheet, while the F1 key will make another worksheet for the new chart.

Shortcut #84: Shift + F11

This is an alternative to Shortcut #59: Alt + Shift + F1, wherein it will insert a new worksheet.

Shortcut #85: Alt + F11

Alt + F11 will open the Microsoft Visual Basic Editor. In this menu, you can create or edit a macro by using the Visual Basic for Applications (VBA) programming language.

Shortcut #86: F12

The F12 key is the shortcut for the Save As dialog box. It lets you save your Excel file among the available formats.

In case you're wondering why the F1, F4, F6 and F10 keys as well as some of their derivatives are not included in the list, these function keys have already been discussed in the previous chapters. Moreover, as this book specifically claims that it will contain at least a hundred keyboard shortcuts, putting these function keys again in the list will not create an accurate count of all the shortcuts.

Chapter 5: Discovering Ctrl Combinations

There are more than 50 Ctrl key combinations that you can use in the Excel sheet, with some shortcuts comprising of special characters instead of the usual alphanumeric ones. Thus, it would be unpractical to include every possible shortcut, especially if there's a little chance that a typical user will use them all.

With these reasons, only the f14 most valuable Ctrl shortcuts will be contained in the list below.

Shortcut #87: Ctrl + ;

Ctrl + ; will show the current date in the active cell.

Shortcut #88: Ctrl + Shift + #

Ctrl + Shift + # will change the date into a day-month-year format.

Shortcut #89: Ctrl + A

This is an alternative to Shortcut #13: Ctrl + Shift + Spacebar. Pressing these keys will also select the whole worksheet.

Shortcut #90: Ctrl + C

Ctrl + C will copy the contents of the active cell.

Shortcut #91: Ctrl + F

If you need to search for a specific data, you don't have to go to the Home tab and choose Find & Select. By pressing Ctrl + F, you can now access the Find and Replace dialog box immediately.

Shortcut #92: Ctrl + K

To insert or edit a hyperlink, use this shortcut.

Shortcut #93: Ctrl + R

This activates the Fill Right command. To use this, simply click on a cell you want filled then press Ctrl + R. It will copy all the formatting and contents of the cell to its left.

Shortcut #94: Ctrl + S

Ctrl + S will automatically save your file in its current name, location and format.

Shortcut #95: Ctrl + V

After doing Shortcut #90: Ctrl + C, you then proceed with Ctrl + V to paste the contents that you have copied.

Shortcut #96: Ctrl + Alt + V

Since the above shortcut will paste all the data as is, the Ctrl + Alt + V will give you most pasting options as it will open the Paste Special dialog box.

Shortcut #97: Ctrl + W

This combination is an alternative to Shortcut #66: Ctrl + F4, which closes the Excel program.

Shortcut #98: Ctrl + X

This will cut the contents of an active cell. When you say "cut", it will remove the data in a cell and will place it temporarily in the Clipboard so that you can paste the contents in another cell.

Shortcut #99: Ctrl + Y

The Ctrl + Y shortcut runs the Redo function, which means that it will repeat the previous command that you have done.

Shortcut #100: Ctrl + Z

Lastly, Ctrl + Z serve as the shortcut for the Undo function. This will reverse your latest command in Excel.

And that finishes our countdown for the Top 100 keyboard shortcuts in Microsoft Excel. To wrap things up, the last chapter will provide some pointers in "memorizing" these shortcuts the easiest way.

Chapter 6: Pointers for the Excel Novice

Most people will most likely feel daunted with the mere volume of shortcuts in this book. "How can I ever memorize a hundred of these combinations?", says most people. This fear of memorization only impedes the learning process. As such, you should stay away from this negative thinking.

Practice a Couple of Shortcuts Every Week

To be able to remember these shortcuts effectively, you should use them as often as you could. Have this book by your side always so that you will have a guide as you try to absorb each of these shortcuts. Better yet, you can jot down a couple of shortcuts in a small list so that you can try some of these tricks in your school or the office.

After finishing let's say at least five shortcuts for a week, add another five in the succeeding weeks. Just don't forget the previous shortcuts that you have learned. In no time, you will be able to use these keyboard combinations without the help of a cheat sheet.

Don't Use the Numeric Keypad

Although most people on the go use laptops such as students, many people still use the full-sized keyboard that has a built-in numeric keypad at the right side.

Although several characters in the listed shortcuts are there, the Microsoft Excel does not recognize the use of numeric keypad in its shortcuts. As such, you shouldn't try to practice these shortcuts via the numeric keypad; just use the main keyboard itself.

That ends all the pointers in this guide for Excel shortcuts. With that, you should apply all the learnings that you have discovered through this book in your daily Excel tasks. Hopefully, you'll be a more efficient Excel user as you incorporate these shortcuts in using the said spreadsheet program.

Conclusion

Thank you again for purchasing this book!

I hope this book was able to help you to learn the secrets behind mastering Microsoft Excel, which are the 100 keyboard shortcuts.

The next step is to make use of these shortcuts every time you operate on the Excel application. Through this, you can now easily work on your Excel spreadsheets with only a minimal use of a mouse.

Finally, if you enjoyed this book, please take the time to share your thoughts and post a review on Amazon. We do our best to reach out to readers and provide the best value we can. Your positive review will help us achieve that. It'd be greatly appreciated!

Thank you and good luck!

Book 2
PHP Programming Professional Made Easy

BY SAM KEY

Expert PHP Programming Language Success in a Day for any Computer User!

Table of Contents

Introduction

I want to thank you and congratulate you for purchasing the book, "Professional PHP Programming Made Easy: Expert PHP Programming Language Success in a Day for any Computer User!"

This book contains proven steps and strategies on how to quickly transition from client side scripting to server side scripting using PHP.

The book contains a condensed version of all the topics you need to know about PHP as a beginner. To make it easier for you to understand the lessons, easy to do examples are included.

If you are familiar with programming, it will only take you an hour or two to master the basics of PHP. If you are new to programming, expect that you might take two to three days to get familiar with this great server scripting language.

Thanks again for purchasing this book, I hope you enjoy it!

Chapter 1: Setting Expectations and Preparation

PHP is a scripting language primarily used by web developers to create interactive and dynamic websites. This book will assume that you are already familiar with HTML and CSS. By the way, a little bit of XML experience is a plus.

This book will also assume that you have a good understanding and experience with JavaScript since most of the explanations and examples here will use references to that client side scripting language

To be honest, this will be like a reference book to PHP that contains bits of explanations. And since JavaScript is commonly treated as a prerequisite to learning PHP, it is expected that most web developers will experience no difficulty in shifting to using this server side scripting language.

However, if you have little knowledge of JavaScript or any other programming language, expect that you will have a steep learning curve if you use this book. Nevertheless, it does not mean that it is impossible to learn PHP without a solid background in programming or client side scripting. You just need to play more with the examples presented in this book to grasp the meaning and purpose of the lessons.

Anyway, unlike JavaScript or other programming languages, you cannot just test PHP codes in your computer. You will need a server to process it for you. There are three ways to do that:

1. Get a web hosting account. Most web hosting packages available on the web are PHP ready. All you need to do is code your script, save it as .php or .htm, upload it to your web directory, and access it.

2. Make your computer as simple web server. You can do that by installing a web server application in your computer. If your computer is running on Microsoft Windows, you can install XAMPP to make your computer act like a web server. Do not worry. Your computer will be safe since your XAMPP, by default, will make your computer only available to your use.

3. Use an online source code editor that can execute PHP codes. Take note that this will be a bit restricting since most of them only accept and execute PHP codes. It means that you will not be able to mix HTML, CSS, JavaScript, and PHP in one go. But if you are going to study the basics, which the lessons in this book are all about, it will be good enough.

Chapter 2: PHP Basics

This chapter will teach you the primary things that you need to know when starting to code PHP. It includes PHP's syntax rules, variables, constants, echo and print, operators, and superglobals.

Syntax

PHP code can be placed anywhere in an HTML document or it can be saved in a file with .php as its file extension. Just like JavaScript, you will need to enclose PHP code inside tags to separate it from HTML. The tag will tell browsers that all the lines inside it are PHP code.

PHP's opening tag is <?php and its closing tag is ?>. For example:

```
<!DOCTYPE html>
</html>
<head></head>
<body>
	<h1>Heading for the page</h2>
	<p>Some paragraph</p>
	<?php
		// Insert some PHP code in here.
	?>
</body>
</html>
```

Echo and Print

PHP code blocks do not only return the values you requested from them, but you can also let it return HTML or text to the HTML file that invoked the PHP code blocks. To do that, you will need to use the echo or print command. Below are samples on how they can be used:

```
<?php
echo "Hello World!";
?>
<?php
print "Hello World!";
?>
```

Once the browser parses that part of the HTML, that small code will be processed on the server, and the server will send the value "Hello World" back to the client. Browsers handle echo and print values by placing them in the HTML file code. It will appear after the HTML element where the PHP code was inserted. For example:

```
<p>This is a paragraph.</p>
<?php
echo "Hello World!";
?>
<p>This is another paragraph.</p>
```

Once the browser parses those lines, this will be the result:

This is a paragraph.

Hello World!

This is another paragraph.

You can even echo HTML elements. For example:

```
<p>P1.</p>
<?php
print "<a href='http://www.google.com' >Google</a>";
?>
<p>P2.</p>
```

As you have witnessed, both echo and print have identical primary function, which is to send output to the browser. They have two differences however. Print can only handle one parameter while echo can handle multiple parameters. Another difference is that you can use print in expressions since it returns a value of 1 while you cannot use echo. Below is a demonstration of their differences:

```
<?php
echo "Hello World!", "How are you?";
?>
<?php
print "Hello World!", "How are you?";
?>
```

The echo code will be successfully sent to the client, but the print code will bring up a syntax error due to the unexpected comma (,) and the additional parameter or value after it. Though, if you want to use print with multiple parameters, you can concatenate the values of the parameters instead. String concatenation will be discussed later.

```
<?php
$x = 1 + print("test");
echo $x;
?>
<?php
$x = 1 + echo("test");
echo $x;
?>
```

The variable $x will have a value of 2 since the expression print("test") will return a value of 1. Also, even it is used as a value in an expression, the print command will still produce an output.

On the other hand, the echo version of the code will return a syntax error due to the unexpected appearance of echo in the expression.

Many web developers use the echo and print commands to provide dynamic web content for small and simple projects. In advanced projects, using return to send an array of variables that contain HTML content and displaying them using JavaScript or any client side scripting is a much better method.

Variables

Creating a variable in JavaScript requires you to declare it and use the keyword var. In PHP, you do not need to declare to create a variable. All you need to do is assign a value in a variable for it to be created. Also, variables in PHP always starts with a dollar sign ($).

```
<?php
$examplevariable = "Hello World!";
echo $examplevariable;
?>
```

There are rules to follow when creating a variable, which are similar to JavaScript's variable syntax.

- The variable's name or identifier must start with a dollar sign ($).
- An underscore or a letter must follow it.

- Placing a number or any symbol after the dollar sign instead will return a syntax error.
- The identifier must only contain letters, numbers, or underscores.
- Identifiers are case sensitive. The variable $x is treated differently from $X.

You can assign any type of data into a PHP variable. You can store strings, integers, floating numbers, and so on. If you have experienced coding using other programming languages, you might be thinking where you would need to declare the data type of the variable. You do not need to do that. PHP will handle that part for you. All you need to do is to assign the values in your variables.

Variable Scopes

Variables in PHP also change their scope, too, depending on the location where you created them.

Local

If you create a variable inside a function, it will be treated as a local variable. Unlike JavaScript, assigning a value to variable for the first time inside a function will not make them global due to way variables are created in PHP.

Global

If you want to create global variables, you can do it by creating a value outside your script's functions. Another method is to use the global keyword. The global keyword can let you create or access global variables inside a function. For example:

```
<?php
function test() {
	global $x;
	$x = "Hello World!";
}
test();
echo $x;
?>
```

In the example above, the line global $x defined variable $x as a global variable. Because of that, the echo command outside the function was able to access $x without encountering an undefined variable error.

As mentioned a while ago, you can use the global keyword to access global variables inside functions. Below is an example:

```
<?php
$x = "Hello Word!";
function test() {
        global $x;
        echo $x;
}
test();
?>
```

Just like before, the command echo will not encounter an error as long as the global keyword was used for the variable $x.

Another method you can use is to access your script's global values array, $GLOBALS. With $GLOBALS, you can create or access global values. Here is the previous example used once again, but with the $GLOBALS array used instead of the global keyword:

```
<?php
function test() {
        $GLOBALS['x'] = "Hello World!";
}
test();
echo $x;
?>
```

Take note that when using $GLOBALS, you do not need the dollar sign when creating or accessing a variable.

Static

If you are not comfortable in using global variables just to keep the values that your functions use, you can opt to convert your local variables to static. Unlike local variables, static variables are not removed from the memory once the function that houses them ends. They will stay in the memory like global variables, but they will be only accessible on the functions they reside in. For example:

```
<?php
```

```
function test() {
	static $y = 1;
	if (empty($y))
		{$y = 1;}
	echo $y . " ";
	$y += $y;
}
test();
test();
test();
test();
test();
?>
```

In the example, the variable $y's value is expected to grow double as the function is executed. With the help of static keyword, the existence and value of $y is kept in the script even if the function where it serves as a local variable was already executed.

As you can see, together with the declaration that the variable $y is static, the value of 1 was assigned to it. The assignment part in the declaration will only take effect during the first time the function was called and the static declaration was executed.

Superglobals

PHP has predefined global variables. They contain values that are commonly accessed, define, and manipulated in everyday server side data execution. Instead of manually capturing those values, PHP has placed them into its predefined superglobals to make the life of PHP programmers easier.

- **$GLOBALS**
- **$_SERVER**
- **$_REQUEST**
- **$_POST**
- **$_GET**
- **$_FILES**

- $_ENV
- $_COOKIE
- $_SESSION

SUPERGLOBALS HAVE CORE USES IN PHP SCRIPTING. YOU WILL BE MOSTLY USING ONLY FIVE OF THESE SUPERGLOBALS IN YOUR EARLY DAYS IN CODING PHP. THEY ARE: $GLOBALS, $_SERVER, $_REQUEST, $_POST, AND $_GET.

Constants

Constants are data storage containers just like variables, but they have global scope and can be assigned a value once. Also, the method of creating a constant is much different than creating a variable. When creating constants, you will need to use the define() construct. For example:

```
<?php
define(this_is_a_constant, “the value”, false);
?>
```

The define() construct has three parameters: define(name of constant, value of the constant, is case sensitive?). A valid constant name must start with a letter or an underscore – you do not need to place a dollar sign ($) before it. Aside from that, all other naming rules of variables apply to constants.

The third parameter requires a Boolean value. If the third parameter was given a true argument, constants can be accessed regardless of their case or capitalization. If set to false, its case will be strict. By default, it will be set to false.

Operators

By time, you must be already familiar with operators, so this book will only refresh you about them. Fortunately, the usage of operators in JavaScript and PHP is almost similar.

- Arithmetic: +, -, *, /, %, and **.
- Assignment: =, +=, -=, *=, /=, and %=.
- Comparison: ==, ===, !=, <>, !==, >, <, >=, and <=.

- Increment and Decrement: ++x, x++, --x, and x--.
- Logical: and, or, xor, &&, ||, and !.
- String: . and .=.
- Array: +, ==, ===, !=, <>, and !==.

Chapter 3: Flow Control

Flow control is needed when advancing or creating complex projects with any programming language. With them, you can control the blocks of statements that will be executed in your script or program. Most of the syntax and rules in the flow control constructs in PHP are almost similar to JavaScript, so you will not have a hard time learning to use them in your scripts.

Functions

Along the way, you will need to create functions for some of the frequently repeated procedures in your script. Creating functions in PHP is similar to JavaScript. The difference is that function names in PHP are not case sensitive. For example:

```
<?php
function test($parameter = "no argument input") {
	print $parameter;
}
TEST("Success!");
tEsT();
?>
```

In JavaScript, calling a function using its name in different casing will cause an error. With PHP, you will encounter no problems or errors as long as the spelling of the name is correct.

Also, did you notice the variable assignment on the sample function's parameter? The value assigned to the parameter's purpose is to provide a default value to it when the function was called without any arguments being passed for the parameter.

In the example, the second invocation of the function test did not provide any arguments for the function to assign to the $parameter. Because of that, the value 'no argument input' was assigned to $parameter instead.

In JavaScript, providing a default value for a parameter without any value can be tricky and long depending on the number of parameters that will require default arguments or parameter values.

Of course, just like JavaScript, PHP functions also return values with the use of the return keyword.

If, Else, and Elseif Statements

PHP has the same if construct syntax as JavaScript. To create an if block, start by typing the if keyword, and then follow it with an expression to be evaluated inside parentheses. After that, place the statements for your if block inside curly braces. Below is an example:

```
<?php
$color1 = "blue";
if ($color1 == "blue") {
	echo "The color is blue! Yay!";
}
?>
```

If you want your if statement to do something else if the condition returns a false, you can use else.

```
<?php
$color1 = "blue";
if ($color1 == "blue") {
	echo "The color is blue! Yay!";
}
else {
	echo "The color is not blue, you liar!";
}
?>
```

In case you want to check for more conditions in your else statements, you can use elseif instead nesting an if statement inside else. For example:

```
<?php
$color1 = "blue";
if ($color1 == "blue") {
	echo "The color is blue! Yay!";
}
else {
	if ($color == "green") {
		echo "Hmm. I like green, too. Yay!";
	}
	else {
```

```
        echo "The color is not blue, you liar!";
    }
}
?>
```

Is the same as:

```
<?php
$color1 = "blue";
if ($color1 == "blue") {
    echo "The color is blue! Yay!";
}
elseif ($color == "green" {
    echo "Hmm. I like green, too. Yay!";}
else {
    echo "The color is not blue, you liar!";
}
?>
```

Using elseif is less messy and is easier to read.

Switch Statement

However, if you are going to check for multiple conditions for one expression or variable and place a lot of statements per condition satisfied, it is better to use switch than if statements. For example, the previous if statement is the same as:

```
<?php
$color1 = "blue";
switch ($color1) {
    case "blue":
        echo "The color is blue! Yay!";
        break;
    case "green":
        echo "Hmm. I like green, too. Yay!";
        break;
    case default:
        echo "The color is not blue, you liar!";
}
?>
```

The keyword switch starts the switch statement. Besides it is the value or expression that you will test. It must be enclosed in parentheses.

Every case keyword entry must be accompanied with the value that you want to compare against the expression being tested. Each case statement can be translated as if <expression 1> is equal to <expression 2>, and then perform the statements below.

The break keyword is used to signal the script that the case block is over and the any following statements after it should not be done.

On the other hand, the default case will be executed when no case statements were satisfied by the expression being tested.

Chapter 4: Data Types – Part 1

PHP also has the same data types that you can create and use in other programming languages. Some of the data types in PHP have different ways of being created and assigned from the data types in JavaScript.

Strings

Any character or combination of characters placed in double or single quotes are considered strings in PHP. In PHP, you will deal with text a lot more often than other programming languages. PHP is used typically to handle data going from the client to the server and vice versa. Due to that, you must familiarize yourself with a few of the most common used string operators and methods.

Numbers

Integer

Integers are whole numbers without fractional components or values after the decimal value. When assigning or using integers in PHP, it is important that you do not place blanks and commas between them to denote or separate place values.

An integer value can be positive, negative or zero. In PHP, you can display integers in three forms: decimal (base 10), octal (base 8), or hexadecimal (base 16). To denote that a value is in hexadecimal form, always put the prefix 0x (zero-x) with the value (e.g., 0x1F, 0x4E244D, 0xFF11AA). On the other hand, to denote that a value is in octal form, put the prefix 0 (zero) with the value (e.g., 045, 065, and 0254).

If you echo or print an integer variable, its value will be automatically presented in its decimal form. In case that you want to show it in hexadecimal or octal you can use dechex() or decoct() respectively. For example:

```
<?php
echo dechex(255);
echo decoct(9);
?>
```

The first echo will return FF, which is 255 in decimal. The second echo will return 11, which is 9 in octal. As you might have noticed, the prefix 0x and 0 were not present in the result. The prefixes only apply when you write those two presentations of integers in your script.

On the other hand, you can use hexdec() to reformat a hexadecimal value to decimal and use octdec() to reformat an octal value to decimal.

You might think of converting hex to oct or vice versa. Unfortunately, PHP does not have constructs like hexoct() or octhex(). To perform that kind of operation, you will need to manually convert the integer to decimal first then convert it to hex or oct.

Float or Double

Floating numbers are real numbers (or approximations of real numbers). In other words, it can contain fractional decimal values.

Since integers are a subset of real numbers, integers are floating numbers. Just adding a decimal point and a zero to an integer in PHP will make PHP consider that the type of the variable that will store that value is float instead of integer.

Boolean

Boolean is composed of two values: True and False. In PHP, true and false are not case sensitive. Both values are used primarily in conditional statements, just like in JavaScript.

Also, false is equivalent to null, a blank string, and 0 while true is equivalent to any number except 0 or any string that contains at least one character.

NULL

This is a special value type. In case that a variable does not contain a value from any other data types, it will have a NULL value instead. For example, if you try to access a property from an object that has not been assigned a value yet, it will have a NULL value. By the way, you can assign NULL to variables, too.

Resource

RESOURCES IS A SPECIAL VARIABLE TYPE. THEY ONLY SERVE AS A REFERENCE TO EXTERNAL RESOURCE AND ARE ONLY CREATED BY SPECIAL FUNCTIONS. AN EXAMPLE OF A RESOURCE IS A DATABASE LINK.

Chapter 5: Data Types – Part 2

The data types explained in this chapter are essential to your PHP programming life. In other programming languages, you can live without this data types. However, in PHP, you will encounter them most of the time, especially if you will start to learn and use databases on your scripts.

ARRAYS

Arrays are data containers for multiple values. You can store numbers, strings, and even arrays in an array. Array in PHP is a tad different in JavaScript, so it will be discussed in detail in this book.

There are three types of array in PHP: indexed, associative, and multidimensional.

Indexed Arrays

Indexed array is the simplest form of arrays in PHP. For those people who are having a hard time understanding arrays, think of an array as a numbered list that starts with zero. To create or assign values to an array, you must use the construct array(). For example:

```
<?php
$examplearray = array(1, 2, "three");
?>
```

To call values inside an array, you must call them using their respective indices. For example:

```
<?php
$examplearray = array(1, 2, "three");
echo $examplearray[0];
echo $examplearray['2'];
?>
```

The first echo will reply with 1 and the second echo will reply three. As you can see, in indexed arrays, you can call values with just a number or a number inside quotes. When dealing with indexed arrays, it is best that you use the first method.

Since the number 1 was the first value to be assigned to the array, index 0 was assigned to it. The index number of the values in an array increment by 1. So, the index numbers of the values 2 and three are 1 and 2 respectively.

Associative Arrays

The biggest difference between associative arrays and indexed arrays is that you can define the index keys of the values in associative arrays. The variable $GLOBALS is one of the best example of associative arrays in PHP. To create an associative array, follow the example:

```
<?php
$examplearray = array("indexo" => "John", 2 => "Marci");
echo $examplearray["indexo"];
echo $examplearray[2];
?>
```

The first echo will return John and the second echo will return Marci. Take note that if you use associative array, the values will not have indexed numbers.

Multidimensional Arrays

Multidimensional arrays can store values, indexed arrays, and associative arrays. If you create an array in your script, the $GLOBALS variable will become a multidimensional array. You can insert indexed or associative arrays in multidimensional arrays. However, take note that the same rules apply to their index keys. To create one, follow the example below:

```
<?php
$examplearray = array(array("test1", 1, 2), array("test2" =>
3, "test3" => 4), array("test4", 5, 6));
echo $examplearray[1]["test2"];
echo $examplearray[1][1];
echo $examplearray[2][0];
?>
```

As you can see, creating multidimensional arrays is just like nesting arrays on its value. Calling values from multidimensional is simple.

If a value was assigned, it can be called like a regular array value using its index key. If a value was paired with a named key, it can be called by its name. If an array was assigned, you can call the value inside it by calling the index key of the array first, and then the index key of the value inside it.

In the example, the third echo called the array in index 2 and accessed the value located on its 0 index. Hence, it returned test4.

Objects

Objects are like small programs inside your script. You can assign variables within them called properties. You can also assign functions within them called methods.

Creating and using objects can make you save hundreds of lines of code, especially if you have some bundle of codes that you need to use repeatedly on your scripts. To be on the safe side, the advantages of using objects depend on the situation and your preferences.

Debates about using objects in their scripts (object oriented programming) or using functions (procedural programming) instead have been going on forever. It is up to you if you will revolve your programs around objects or not.

Nevertheless, to create objects, you must create a class for them first. Below is an example on how to create a class in PHP.

```
<?php
class Posts {
	function getPost() {
		$this->post1 = "Post Number 1.";
	}
	var $post2 = "Post Number 2.";
}

$test = new Posts();
echo $test->post2;
$test->getPost();
echo $test->post1;
?>
```

In this example, a new class was created using the class keyword. The name of the class being created is Posts. In class declarations, you can create functions that will be methods for the objects under the class. And you can create variables that will be properties for the subjects under the class.

First, a function was declared. If the function was called, it will create a property for an object under the Posts class called post1. Also, a value was assigned to it. You might have noticed the $this part in the declaration inside the function. The $this variable represents the object that owns the function being declared.

Besides it is a dash and a chevron (->). Some programmers informally call it as the instance operator. This operator allows access to the instances (methods and properties) of an object. In the statement, the script is accessing the post1 property inside the $this object, which is the object that owns the function. After accessing the property, the statement assigned a value to it.

Aside from the function or method declaration, the script created a property called post2, which is a variable owned by the Posts class. To declare one, you need to use the keyword var (much like in JavaScript). After this statement, the class declaration ends.

The next statement contains the variable assignment, $test = new Posts(). Technically, that means that the variable $test will become a new object under the Posts class. All the methods and properties that was declared inside the Posts() class declaration will be given to it.

To test if the $test class became a container for a Posts object, the script accessed the property post2 from $test and then echoed it to produce an output. The echo will return , 'Post number 2.'. Indeed, the $test variable is already an object under the Posts class.

What if you call and print the property post1 from the variable $test? It will not return anything since it has not been created or initialized yet. To make it available, you need to invoke the getPost() method of $test. Once you do, you will be able to access the property post1.

And that is just the tip of the iceberg. You will be working more on objects on advanced PHP projects.

Conclusion

Thank you again for purchasing this book!

I hope this book was able to help you to learn PHP fast.

The next step is to:

Learn the other superglobals

Learn from handling in HTML, JavaScript, and PHP

Learn using MySQL

Finally, if you enjoyed this book, please take the time to share your thoughts and post a review on Amazon. We do our best to reach out to readers and provide the best value we can. Your positive review will help us achieve that. It'd be greatly appreciated!

Thank you and good luck!

Check Out My Other Books

Below you'll find some of my other popular books that are popular on Amazon and Kindle as well. Simply click on the links below to check them out. Alternatively, you can visit my author page on Amazon to see other work done by me.

Android Programming in a Day

Python Programming in a Day

C Programming Success in a Day

CSS Programming Professional Made Easy

C Programming Professional Made Easy

JavaScript Programming Made Easy

Windows 8 Tips for Beginners

Windows 8 Tips for Beginners

HTML Professional Programming Made Easy

C ++ Programming Success in a Day

If the links do not work, for whatever reason, you can simply search for these titles on the Amazon website to find them.

www.ingramcontent.com/pod-product-compliance
Lightning Source LLC
Chambersburg PA
CBHW061039050326
40689CB00012B/2896
* 9 7 8 1 5 1 8 6 1 2 3 0 5 *